P9-ANY-317

STEP BY STEP PROJECTS

How to Make a TERRARIUM

Jeff Barger

rourkeeducationalmedia.com

Before & After Reading Activities

Teaching Focus: Teacher-child conversations: Teacher-child conversations play an important role in shaping what children learn. Practice this and see how these conversations help scaffold your student's learning.

Before Reading:

Building Academic Vocabulary and Background Knowledge

Before reading a book, it is important to set the stage for your child or student by using pre-reading strategies. This will help them develop their vocabulary, increase their reading comprehension, and make connections across the curriculum.

1. Read the title and look at the cover. *Let's make predictions about what this book will be about.*
2. Take a picture walk by talking about the pictures/photographs in the book. Implant the vocabulary as you take the picture walk. Be sure to talk about the text features such as headings, Table of Contents, glossary, bolded words, captions, charts/ diagrams, or Index.
3. Have students read the first page of text with you then have students read the remaining text.
4. Strategy Talk – use to assist students while reading.
   - Get your mouth ready
   - Look at the picture
   - Think…does it make sense
   - Think…does it look right
   - Think…does it sound right
   - Chunk it – by looking for a part you know
5. Read it again.
6. After reading the book complete the activities below.

Content Area Vocabulary
Use glossary words in a sentence.

container
direct
indirect
layer
magnifies
terrarium

After Reading:

Comprehension and Extension Activity

After reading the book, work on the following questions with your child or students in order to check their level of reading comprehension and content mastery.

1. *How do you build a terrarium?* (Summarize)
2. *What is direct sunlight?* (Asking Questions)
3. *According to the text, which object do you place on the bottom layer of a terrarium?* (Asking Questions)
4. *Have you planted a garden before? If so, what did you plant?* (Text to Self Connection)

Extension Activity

As a class, create a terrarium. Decide where the best location in the classroom would be. Does this space have direct or indirect sunlight? Add one layer of material each day. Brainstorm why each layer is necessary for the terrarium.

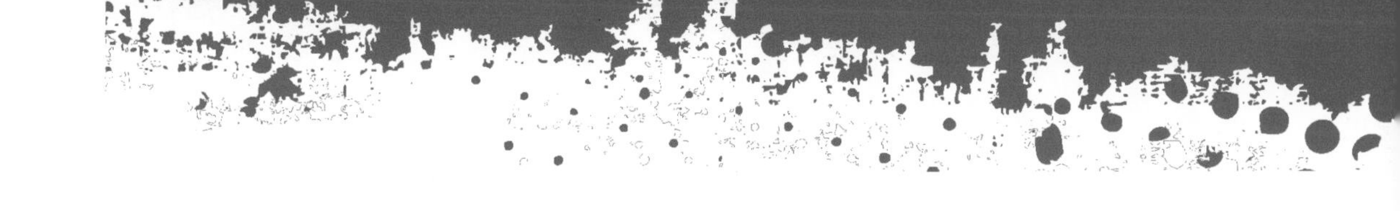

Table of Contents

Grow an Indoor Garden

Can a garden grow inside?

Yes! It is called a **terrarium.** It is small and easy to care for.

Terrariums can be open or closed at the top.

You will need:

glass **container**

small rocks

potting soil

sheet moss

plants

decoration

scissors

spoon

Choosing a Home

Find a clear glass container. Your hand should fit in the opening. Is it deep enough for the plant roots?

Where do you place your terrarium? Does the spot have **direct** or **indirect** sunlight?

If an object gets sunlight directly, it will heat up more than if it gets sunlight at an angle.

Glass **magnifies.** Direct sunlight will make it too hot for some plants. Check the plant tag. It will tell you the best amount of sunlight needed for your plants to grow.

Planting the Plants

Make a **layer** of rocks on the bottom. One to two inches (2.5 to 5 centimeters) should be enough.

Dip sheet moss in water for a few seconds.

Cover the rocks.

Next, spoon potting soil over the moss. Start with a three inch (7.62 centimeter) layer of soil. Adjust as needed.

For All
FOR
ORGANIC
For Indoor &
All Natural

What will you grow in your terrarium? Pick plants that will not grow too big. Brush off your plants before planting. Check for bugs too!

If you choose cacti or succulents, make sure your container is open. Pick plants that can tolerate high humidity if the container is closed.

Make a hole for the plant in the soil. Place the plant and cover the roots with soil. Pat the soil. Add a small amount of water.

Final Touches

You can add small figures to your terrarium. Add a miniature house or plastic animals!

Follow plant instructions for watering. Enjoy your new garden!

Photo Glossary

container (kuhn-TAY-ner): An object, such as a box, jar, or barrel, that is used to hold something.

direct (duh-REKT): Moving or laid out in a straight line.

indirect (in-duh-REKT): Not in a straight line.

layer (LAY-ur): A thickness or coating of something.

magnifies (MAG-nuh-fies): Makes something seem bigger, more important, or more effective.

terrarium (tuh-RAIR-ee-uhm): A glass or plastic container for growing small plants or raising small land animals.

Index

Further Reading

Bradley, Val, *Bring the Outside In,* Transworld Publishers, 2018.
Colletti, Maria, *Terrariums: Gardens Under Glass,* Cool Springs Press, 2015.
Felix, Rebecca, *Mini Decorating*, Lerner, 2017.

About the Author

Jeff Barger is a literacy specialist who lives in North Carolina. He thinks a Venus Flytrap in a terrarium would be really cool.

www.rourkeeducationalmedia.com

PHOTO CREDITS: All photography by Blue Door Education except the following images © Shutterstock.com: pages 4-5 By tarapong srichaiyos, page 6 glass container By rangizzz, rocks By Funnyjoke, potting soil By imstock, scissors By Hurst Photo, spoon, By onair; page 10 By Myimagine; page 11 photo By Krisana Antharith, illustration By Julia Musdotter; page 17 By Konstantins Pobilojs

Edited by: Keli Sipperley

Produced by Blue Door Education for Rourke Educational Media.
Cover and page design: by Nicola Stratford
www.nicolastratford.com

Library of Congress PCN Data

How to Make a Terrarium / Jeff Barger
(Step-By-Step Projects)
ISBN 978-1-64156-428-1 (hard cover)
ISBN 978-1-64156-554-7 (soft cover)
ISBN 978-1-64156-675-9 (e-Book)
Library of Congress Control Number: 2018930448

Rourke Educational Media
Printed in the United States of America, North Mankato, Minnesota